THE FUNNY
CHRISTMAS
STOCKING-FILLER
BOOK

THE FUNNY
CHRISTMAS
STOCKING-FILLER
BOOK

BY JONATHAN SWAN

EBURY
PRESS

1 3 5 7 9 10 8 6 4 2

Ebury Press is an imprint of Ebury Publishing,
20 Vauxhall Bridge Road, London SW1V 2SA

Ebury Press is part of the Penguin Random House group of companies whose
addresses can be found at global.penguinrandomhouse.com

Penguin
Random House
UK

Copyright © Ebury Publishing 2016

First published by Ebury Press in 2016

Reissued by Ebury Press in 2019

www.penguin.co.uk

A CIP catalogue record for this book is available from the British Library

ISBN 9781529105124

Printed and bound in Great Britain by Clays Ltd, Elcograf S.p.A.

Penguin Random House is committed to a
sustainable future for our business, our readers
and our planet. This book is made from Forest
Stewardship Council® certified paper.

'I am sorry to have to introduce the subject of Christmas. It is an indecent subject; a cruel, gluttonous subject; a drunken, disorderly subject; a wasteful, disastrous subject; a wicked, cadging, lying, filthy, blasphemous and demoralizing subject. Christmas is forced on a reluctant and disgusted nation by the shopkeepers and the press: on its own merits it would wither and shrivel in the fiery breath of universal hatred; and anyone who looked back to it would be turned into a pillar of greasy sausages.'

GEORGE BERNARD SHAW

IT'S CHRISTMAS!

Welcome to the *Funny Christmas Stocking Filler Book*. Part survival guide, part instruction manual, part trivia trove, this handy tome is all you need to navigate Christmas successfully. Christmas comes but once a year, although it is super-sizing like a teenager in McDonalds. From Autumn onwards it barrels towards us, yet it still catches us out: presents remain unbought until the last minute, trees are hastily dragged home on Christmas Eve and the lights never work, even though they did when they were packed away. Your in-laws, as welcome as an incoming warhead, are on their approach trajectory, and the dog keeps trying to mount the defrosting turkey. It isn't like this in the John Lewis adverts.

So turn to this book for comfort and advice. Why not suggest a few classic Christmas games, or whip up a Christmas drink to lubricate festivities? Try a Christmas quiz, and see who is the real Christmas fanatic. Or you could just take your new copy and go and read it in the loo for half an hour while everyone shouts at each other after lunch.

Finally, if you are reading this in a bookshop on Christmas Eve with only 40 mins until the shops close and gifts left to buy, you're holding your salvation right in your clammy hands. Grab five copies, march to the till and pay. Sorted. You're welcome. Happy Christmas, that's our gift to you!

Did you know?

XMAS OR CHRISTMAS?

The common abbreviation for Christmas to Xmas is derived from the Greek alphabet. X is letter Chi, which is the first letter of Christ's name in the Greek alphabet.

Although its use is frowned upon by the BBC and *The Times*, for example, Xmas isn't some modern abbreviation that has come into use relatively recently. In fact, the earliest recorded instance can be found almost 1,000 years ago. There may have been good reasons for abbreviating Christmas to Xmas: parchment and vellum that scribes wrote on was expensive stuff, and so saving space and cramming more words in would have saved a little bit of money.

HIDE THE PICKLE

In Germany there is an old tradition of hiding a pickle in the tree on Christmas Eve. The first child to find it the next morning gets an extra gift.

Sounds plausible and authentic? Then try asking a German about this well-known 'tradition' and you'll be met with an uncomprehending stare (at best; a quite serious misunderstanding at worst). The truth is that this myth was probably concocted by canny Christmas decoration sellers in the US in the 1890s, who imported glass ornaments from Germany and came up with the Christmas pickle story, thereby summing up the true spirit of our modern Christmas: selling and buying any old tat.

HOW TO ... GET THROUGH THE OFFICE CHRISTMAS PARTY

Although it gets a bad press, the office Christmas party is a necessity. Like a nasty boil that has to be lanced, the Christmas party releases the tensions that have built up over the year. Understand this and the sight of Kevin from accounts dancing wildly in his pants makes much more sense; what you are actually seeing is a psychological exorcism of a year's worth of Excel spreadsheets. Office parties can be brutal – follow these tips to survive yours:

★ Make sure you are, at worst, the second most drunk person there – no one remembers what that person said or did. It's the person in the number one spot who becomes the legend or cautionary tale.

★ Dress badly. This is not an occasion when you want to look attractive, lest a co-worker make an unwelcome advance. This is one party you want to go home alone from.

★ Minimize risk by getting your 'boss socializing' done early, before either of you has had more than one drink. Or alternatively, get your boss hammered from the get-go and then you can do what you want.

★ Don't suggest games or activities based on your personal interests. Ideas for wet T-shirt contests or scripture quizzes are not going to go down well.

★ Photocopying body parts is never acceptable. However, if you feel compelled to do it, make sure you don't mix up the photocopier with the shredder.

NOVELTY CHRISTMAS SINGLES

Christmas brings out the inner idiot in many. What else can explain that a) people thought it was a good idea to record these songs, and b) other people actually buy them.

1. *'Jingle Bells' – The Singing Dogs* (1955).
   Dogs. 'Singing' Jingle Bells. In reality, a load of barking edited into song form.

2. *'Ding Dong, Ding Ding' – George Harrison* (1974).
   Yes, that George Harrison. The one from the Beatles, and composer of classics like 'My Sweet Lord'. Strangely, this ditty doesn't make it onto his 'Best of' album. Sample lyric: 'Ding dong, ding dong, yesterday, today was tomorrow/ And tomorrow, today will be yesterday'.

3. *'Grandma Got Run Over by a Reindeer' – Elmo and Pats* (1980). In which Grandma, after too much eggnog, falls from a sleigh and is trampled by reindeer. The song managed to incur the wrath of protestors in America, who claimed the song was ageist.

Playlist

4. **'What Are We Going to Get for Er Indoors?' – Dennis Waterman and George Cole** (1983). Singing in character as Terry and Arthur Daley from their 80s TV series *Minder*, this barrel-scraping effort actually made in to Number 21 in the UK charts and stayed in the top 40 for 5 weeks.

5. **'All I Want for Christmas Is My Two Front Teeth' – Spike Jones and His City Slickers** (1948). A song that mocks an unfortunate boy whose Christmas wishes Santa is unable to decipher because his front teeth are missing. A massive hit at the time, and covered by everyone, including the great Nat King Cole!

Weird Traditions

BEATING THE LOG

The Catalonian tradition of *caga tió* (or 'defecating log' in English) involves creating a character out of a small log – often complete with a grinning face and hat – which sits on the dining-room table during the fortnight leading up to Christmas. So far, so weird. But it gets stranger.

The log has to be kept comfortable; it is fed every day with fruit, nuts and sweets, and has a warm blanket put over it. Then on Christmas Eve the entire family beats the log with sticks, while singing traditional songs encouraging the log to poo out gifts. The blanket is then pulled back to reveal a pile of sweets and small presents that the *caga tió* has kindly deposited.

LET IT SNOW

The chances of a white Christmas are just 1 in 10 for England and Wales, and 1 in 6 for Scotland and Northern Ireland.

The coldest Christmas day on record was in 2010 (and it was also the snowiest) with a minimum temperature of -18.2°C, recorded at Altnaharra in Scotland.

The warmest was recorded in 1920 when there was a white (hot) Christmas temperature of 15 degrees in Devon. Climate change is predicted to make the possibility of a white Christmas even scarcer – by 2050 it will be 65% less likely that there will be snow at Christmas in England.

WRAPPING FOR
THE CACK-HANDED

If you must wrap presents, follow this handy guide.
You will need:

★ A massive sheet of wrapping paper, the bigger the
  better, but ideally the size of a bed sheet. 1 piece per
  gift

★ Sticky tape

★ A set of colouring pens

1) Take a gift and place it in the centre of the wrapping sheet.

2) Gather the sheet of paper around the item, sticking it with
   tape as you go.

3) Unpick all the tape when you realise you have used the
   wrapping wrong way up. Start again. Back to 1).

4) Stop for 10 minutes while you fruitlessly pick at the roll of
   tape trying to find the end.

5) Eventually find the tape end and start wrapping.
   Remember – there's no such thing as too much tape.

6) Sit back and admire your wrapping. Notice that a corner of the gift within is poking through the wrapping. Take a coloured pen that best matches the wrapping paper and colour in the protruding corner until it blends in. Sort of.

7) Take present and place it way, way back under the tree where no one will notice.

Take next gift from pile, and repeat.

Top Tip! Away with single-sided sticky tape! Double-sided tape makes even the most cack-handed paper wrangler into a ninja gift wrapper.

Games

PLAY THE QUEEN'S SPEECH BINGO

How many of these words will you spot in the Queen's speech? Make your own set of cards for a fun family game.

☐ OFF
(pronounced 'orf')

☐ ANNUS

☐ WILLIAM

☐ HORSE

☐ ANNE

☐ EUROPE

☐ ENEMIES

☐ LESS

☐ FORTUNATE

☐ GERMAN

☐ FAMILY

☐ LOTTERY

☐ GIN

☐ PRINGLES

☐ BUTLER

☐ FOOTBALL

☐ HAPPY

☐ GRANDCHILD

☐ INTERNET

☐ TWERK

☐ ALAS

☐ BUTTOCK

☐ SHOOTING

☐ GOD

☐ WASTED

CHRISTMAS IN HOLLYWOOD

Match the quotes below to the famous Christmas film…

A. 'Look, Daddy. Teacher says, every time a bell rings an angel gets his wings.'

B. 'You stink! You smell like beef and cheese, you don't smell like Santa.'

C. 'Oh, Vermont should be beautiful this time of the year, with all that snow.'

D. 'Nephew, if I could work my will any idiot who goes around with a Merry Christmas on his lips would be cooked with his own turkey and buried with a stake of holly through his heart.'

E. 'I'm a master of fright, / and a demon of light, / and I'll scare you right out of your pants. / To a guy in Kentucky / I'm Mister Unlucky / And I'm known thoughout England and France / And since I am dead / I can take off my head.'

CHRISTMAS DINNER AROUND THE WORLD

These dishes make sprouts suddenly seem more palatable.

Southern Africa. What could be better than sitting down to a feast of … worms? Mopane worms, to be precise. Fat, and mottled like a granny's hand, these worms are actually the caterpillar of the Emperor moth. Their harvest season is around Christmas, which means they often make it onto the festive menu.

Greenlanders enjoy a heady combo of whale skin and fat and rotted seabird. The whale skin (known as Mattak) is served raw with the fat presented to the diner to be enjoyed, before they turn to the main event of rotten and fermenting seabird. This delicacy, Kiviak, is made by sewing the carcasses of dead auks into the skin of a seal and leaving them to decay for a number of months until good and ripe. Then the seal belly is sliced open and the delicious dead and putrefied birds, feathers and all, are there to savour.

Smalahove, or whole roasted sheep's head, is traditionally
served in **Norway**. The fleece and skin are removed, but the
brains are often left in as a special treat to be spooned out
by the lucky diners. Nothing brings on a sense of wellbeing
and Christmas cheer like a cleanly picked sheep's skull on
the plate. It is traditionally served with aquavit, a potent spirit
that, drunk to excess, numbs the senses. Which makes eating
the brain easier.

WHITE CHRISTMAS

THE bestselling Christmas single ever is Bing Crosby's 'White Christmas', shifting over 50 million copies worldwide. And that's just Bing's version. If you add in all the other recordings by other artists, it's nearer 150 million.

But the song 'White Christmas' didn't make its début in the 1954 film of the same name. It was first heard in 1942's *Holiday Inn*.

Bing had a good ear for a Christmas hit. His unlikely duet with David Bowie on 1982's *The Little Drummer Boy/Peace on Earth* became one of Bowie's best ever selling singles and has been claimed as one of the most successful Christmas duets ever.

> **Bonus fact:** Bing's co-star in the film *White Christmas* was Rosemary Clooney – auntie of George.

Christmas Past

CHRISTMAS LISTS – THEN AND NOW

Compiled by American researchers, this is a list to make frugal parents weep: the top 10 children's most-wanted presents years ago. Expectations were a lot easier to meet back then.

**What children wanted
100 years ago...**   **...and now**

1. Candy   Ditto
2. Nuts   What are these? Get
                                             me more sweets. Now!
3. Rocking horse   Segway
4. Doll   Robot
5. Mittens/gloves   Clothes are not a
                                             present! It's not fair!
6. Toy train   Playstation
7. Oranges   Wtf? Fruit? This is child
                                             abuse.
8. Books   Ipad
9. Handkerchiefs   What are these things?
                                             What do they do?
10. Skates   New Nikes

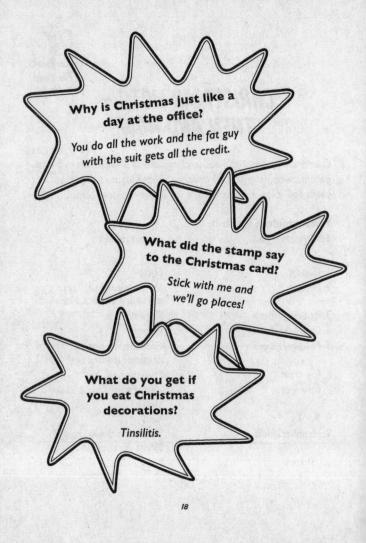

Why is Christmas just like a day at the office?

You do all the work and the fat guy with the suit gets all the credit.

What did the stamp say to the Christmas card?

Stick with me and we'll go places!

What do you get if you eat Christmas decorations?

Tinsilitis.

Survive!

HOW TO ...
HOST A CHRISTMAS PARTY

Hosting a party at Christmas? Don't get caught up in all the fussy to-do lists recommended in the magazines. Who's got time to make mini-Yule logs when there's booze to buy and the worst of the cat sick to clear up? Follow these tricks to make your party swing.

★ Ban children. This is a grown-ups' party. You don't want to be responsible for someone spilling their Chardonnay into a newborn's papoose.

★ Make your place totally Instagrammable. Artful décor, moody lighting, maybe even some celebrity lookalikes. Your guests may be having a rubbish time, but on social media it looks like they were at the best party ever! Isn't that Kanye in the corner?

★ Add a veneer of sophistication by having a drinks trolley. That way you can quickly target alcohol to those bits of the party that seem to be struggling, like a kind of boozy emergency aid drop. Don't have a drinks trolley? A shopping cart filled with cans is fine.

Did you know?

SANTA'S ADDRESS

The true location of Santa's home is something of a mystery. Norwegians believe he's in Drøbak near Oslo, the Danes say he's actually in Greenland, while in Britain, the USA and Canada it's presumed he lives at the North Pole. Finns are adamant the real Santa lives in Lapland. Saint Nicholas, the historic figure who inspired the legend of Santa Claus, actually lived somewhere quite hot. He was born in Turkey, and spent his life there.

> **Extra Santa fact:** In Canada, Santa's postal code is H0H 0H0.

BOY BISHOPS

Even back when the Church was all-powerful, it wasn't all-serious at Christmas.

One tradition that spread throughout medieval Europe was that of the boy bishop. At the beginning of December, usually St Nicholas' day on the 6th, cathedrals chose one of their young choristers to be bishop until Holy Innocents Day on the 28th. Accompanied by a posse of his young choir mates, the newly crowned bishop, resplendent in mitre and robes, travelled round delivering sermons and carrying out all other bishoply duties. People found this extremely amusing and would crowd into churches to see the boy bishop and to watch senior clergy take the place of lowly choristers. The boys were allowed to drink and eat as copiously as they wished. Needless to say, some of the more pious churchmen didn't find it funny at all, but the tradition persisted until the reign of Elizabeth I.

LAST WINTERVAL, I GAVE YOU MY HEART

Bonkers councils replace Christmas with Winterval! The PC Brigade want to kill Christmas! Ever read headlines like these? If you have, you could be forgiven for worrying that Christmas is going to go the way of other significant festivals, like the ancient but now forgotten Lammas Day, and National Richter Scale Day (26 April, since you ask).

It turns out that the plot to replace Christmas with Winterval is a big fat myth. Used originally as a handy way by Birmingham Council to sum up all their festive activities stretching from November to February, it was leapt on and then exaggerated into spurious stories of an attack on Christmas by the media. Worst offenders: *The Times* and the *Daily Mail*.

WHEN IS CHRISTMAS?

Like an aggrieved party host who finds a load of uninvited and unwelcome guests taking over their get-together, pagans accuse Christians of hijacking their festival and ruining it.

Pre-Christian revellers partied hard in December, with the Roman Saturnalia festival on 17 December, the winter solstice on the 21st, followed by the feast of Mithras on the 25th. Christians noticed that everyone was having a good time at this time of year and so decided to declare it the date of the birth of Jesus, which previously had been suggested as anywhere between September and February.

Although Christmas may be superimposed on older pagan festivals, many of their old traditions remain. For example holly, ivy and other greenery, like mistletoe, were gathered by pagans and brought into their houses around the solstice to ward off evil spirits and promote fertility.

HOW TO MAKE
TRADITIONAL EGGNOG

With the texture of phlegm and the colour of bile, eggnog is
a drink traditionally 'enjoyed' over the festive period. It's got a
long history, and Americans were the most enthusiastic early
adopters; the first mention of eggnog is found in a poem in its
honour composed in 1775 by a Maryland preacher. (What is
it with churchmen and booze?)

Eggnog is a staple of the *New York Times* food and drink pages,
going way back to 1895. They've printed various recipes over
the years, but the best one is claimed to be the 1958 version,
devised by Craig Claiborne. Here it is:

INGREDIENTS:

12 eggs, separated;
1 cup granulated sugar;
1 cup bourbon;
1 cup Cognac;
½ teaspoon salt;
3 pints double cream;
grated nutmeg;
1 to 2 cups milk (optional)

METHOD

1. In an electric mixer, beat the egg yolks with the sugar until thick.

2. Slowly add the bourbon and Cognac while beating at slow speed. Chill for several hours.

3. Add the salt to the egg whites. Beat until almost stiff.

4. Whip the cream until stiff.

5. Fold the whipped cream into the yolk mixture, then fold in the beaten egg whites. Chill 1 hour.

6. When ready to serve, sprinkle the top with freshly grated nutmeg. Serve in punch cups with a spoon.

7. If desired, add 1 to 2 cups of milk to the yolk mixture for a thinner eggnog. Makes about 40 punch-cup servings.

Did you know?

REINDEER

Anyone can name all of Santa's reindeer easily.* But did you know these strange facts? Memorise them, and impress your friends with your knowledge of *Rangifer tarandus*.

★ Finns used to measure distance as units of *poronkusema*, which is how far a reindeer can run before having a pee, as they can't run and go at the same time. A *poronkusema* is between 5 and 8 miles, apparently. *Poronkusema* have sadly been washed away by the progress of time, replaced with boring old urine-free units of measurement like miles and kilometres.

★ Reindeer eyes change colour for Christmas. In the summer months their eyes are a golden or brown colour. But as the colder weather sets in, their eyes undergo a complex change and turn blue.

★ Santa's reindeer are all ladies. Rudolph is probably Ruth. Why? Because male reindeer shed their antlers in early winter, way before Christmas comes around.

*Dasher, Dancer, Prancer, Vixen, Comet, Cupid, Donner (thunder), Blitzen (lightning), and that twentieth century interloper Rudolph (Ruth)

26

Weird Traditions

UNGRATEFUL BRATS OF TWITTER

Think good cheer runs like a river through the whole world at Christmas? Not through the Twittersphere it doesn't. Examples of rank ingratitude and oblivious entitlement have been diligently collected by writer Jon Hendren: here are some of the best:

★ 'If I got a black iPad I'd probably kill myself.'

★ 'I'm really not getting an iPhone for Christmas … #heartbreaking #depressing #WHYmom'

★ 'I feel bad for my mom cause I can tell she knows I'm pissed at her for giving me s∗∗∗ ass presents.'

★ 'My stupid Grandma lost my $25 gift voucher. Thanks.'

★ 'Well my guitar finally came, and it sucks, not even the one that I wanted.'

★ 'Didn't get my car so I'm not feeling Christmas …'

★ 'My mom only got me diamond earrings, Odd Future jacket, $30, my mom got a tablet, my brother got a laptop, she lied to me.'

'Christmas at my house is always at least six
or seven times more pleasant than anywhere
else. We start drinking early. And while
everyone else is seeing only one Santa Claus,
we'll be seeing six or seven.'

W.C. FIELDS

BALLOON ANTLERS

A competitive festive game to see who can sprout the biggest set of antlers.

You will need: Minimum two people per team; some pairs of tights with toes cut off (as many as there are teams) uninflated balloons; string or ribbon.

HOW TO PLAY

The aim of the game is to see who can 'grow' the biggest pair of antlers quickest. One player puts the tights on their head. The other team members must blow up the balloons as quickly as they can and stuff them into the legs, tying the toes shut when they have finished. The winners are the team who finished first, or with the tallest antlers. You decide.

CHRISTMAS DELIVERY

According to the figures from the Office of National Statistics fewer babies are born on 25 December than any other day – whether by force of will or simply crossed legs. Overall, 26 September emerges as the most common birthday for people born in England and Wales over the last two decades.

It falls 39 weeks and two days after Christmas Day, meaning that a significant proportion of those born on that day will have been conceived at Christmas itself. Eight of the ten top dates of birth are also towards the end of September, with the remaining two falling at the start of October, suggesting that Christmas cheer fuels an annual spike in autumn births.

Playlist

CHRISTMAS BLUES

Simply having a wonderful Christmas time? Not these unmerry gentlemen. Add these to your Spotify playlist to really get the party started with a ... weep.

★ **'Christmas in Prison'** – John Prine

★ **'Christmas Eve Can Kill You'** – The Everley Brothers

★ **'The Little Boy that Santa Claus Forgot'** – Nat King Cole

★ **'Please, Daddy, Don't Get Drunk This Christmas'** – John Denver

★ **'Another Lonely Christmas'** – Prince

★ **'The Junky's Christmas'** – William Burroughs

★ **'Christmas Without Daddy'** – Loretta Lynn

★ **'Christmas Ain't Like Christmas Anymore'** – Kitty Wells

★ **'Christmas Card from a Hooker in Minneapolis'** – Tom Waits

THE CHRISTMAS LOG

The custom of burning the Yule log goes back to medieval times. Originally a Nordic tradition, Yule is the name of the old winter solstice festivals in Scandinavia and other parts of northern Europe.

The Yule log was originally an entire tree that was carefully chosen and brought into the house with great ceremony. Where this custom came from, nobody is entirely sure, although its roots are probably in ancient pagan beliefs. The largest end of the log would be placed into the hearth while the rest of the tree stuck out into the room! The log would be lit from the remains of the previous year's log, which had been carefully stored away, and slowly fed into the fire through the twelve days of Christmas.

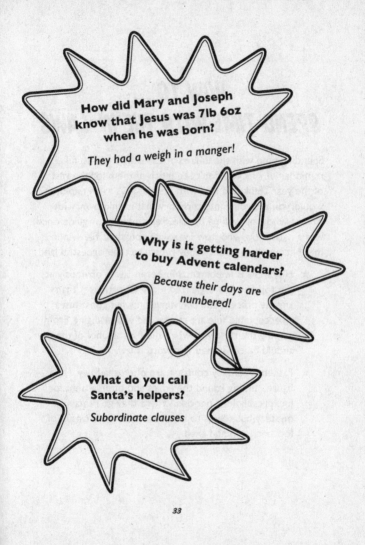

HOW TO ...
SPEND TIME WITH THE IN-LAWS

Spending time with the in-laws at Christmas is a useful reminder of why you don't see much of them for the rest of the year. Think of a stay with your in-laws as an explorer would: you are going into territory that is unknown, with natives who may well be hostile. Remember your guide once was a native too, who now lives with you; their behaviour may become erratic once they return to their ancestral lands.

★ Hierarchy is important. Mother-in-law is obviously at the top. She has organized more Christmases than anyone present and her views on what constitutes an acceptable Yule are strong and wide-ranging. From carving the turkey to when the first alcohol of the day should be consumed, her word is law.

★ Fathers-in-law, by contrast, are often shadowy figures, flitting round the edges and often absent for inexplicably long periods. Where they go remains a mystery but seems to involve an elaborate circuit of loo, bedroom and shed.

★ The experience of spending time with your partner's family is like being dropped into a long-running soap opera, where all the characters have a long and rich shared history. Unfortunately this includes ancient disputes and grievances that can flare up at any time. When this happens, evacuate the immediate vicinity. This is not your fight, and getting involved will happily unite your in-laws but, unhappily, against you.

Games

OPEN IT!!

A game for those people who can't wait to tear open their presents.

You will need: 3–6 players; a wrapped present; hat, coat, scarf and oven gloves; a die.

HOW TO PLAY

Pre-party, wrap up a small gift, then put it in a box and wrap that up. Put the box in an even bigger box and wrap it again. Do this as many times as you have boxes. Think pass the parcel. When wrapping use lots of paper and tough tape – the idea is to make a hard-to-unwrap present.

All the players should sit in a circle and put the wrapped box in the middle. Next to this put the coat, hat, scarf and oven gloves. Take turns rolling the die. As soon as someone rolls a six, they need to put on the coat, hat, scarf and oven gloves and attempt to open the box. In the meantime, the others continue taking turns to roll the die. As soon as the next player rolls a six they take the dressed person's place – taking the coat, hat, scarf and oven gloves and putting them on – and continue tackling the parcel.

Did you know?

BORN TO US THIS DAY

If your birthday is on Christmas day, you're likely to miss out on birthday presents and you can't have a party or go out because everyone's with their family and everywhere is shut. Rubbish. On the upside, you'll probably never have to go to work. Here are some famous people born on Christmas Day...

★ Isaac Newton – the greatest mathematician and physicist

★ Clara Barton – founder of the Red Cross

★ Charles Pathé – French pioneer of film

★ Cab Calloway – band leader and singer

★ Humphrey Bogart – actor, star of *Casablanca*

★ Kenny Everett – TV and radio comedian and presenter

★ Sissy Spacek – actor, played the lead in film *Carrie*

★ Annie Lennox – singer in the Eurythmics

★ Shane MacGowan – singer and composer of Christmas classic '*Fairytale of New York*'

★ Justin Trudeau – Prime Minister of Canada

Food &
Drink

GOBBLE GOBBLE

★ The average weight of of a UK baby is 7.5lb. The average weight of a Christmas turkey is 12lb.

★ The biggest ever turkey weighed in 37.6lbs – roughly the weight of a 3-year-old child. Good luck finding an oven for that (the turkey, not the child).

★ It's estimated that at Christmas in the UK around 6,711 tonnes of fresh turkey and 12,472 tonnes of frozen turkey are cooked. That's almost 20,000 tonnes of meat.

WASSAILING

Not street slang for yachting, wassailing is the original form of the more modern Christmas carol.

A venerable and old custom, it originally toasted the new rising of the sun after the winter solstice. However, by Tudor times it had been upcycled by determined drinkers into a carousing ramble around the village, stopping at every wealthy door and toasting neighbours to a long life. It has a significant advantage over carol singing as it involved the wassail bowl – a big vat containing booze. Wassailers carted this around, stopping off at houses to sing a song and offer a slurp from the wassail bowl in exchange for gifts. Sometimes this was not without a more sinister edge – demands for figgy pudding in 'We Wish You a Merry Christmas' are followed by the menacing refrain 'we won't go until we've got some'. Carolling still goes on, of course, but the custom of the wassail bowl has largely died out. Sadly.

MUST-HAVE MANIA

Every year there's one must-have toy, a plastic Holy Grail. You know Christmas is in full swing when packs of desperate parents roam the shops trying to lay their hands on their little darlings' heart's desire, only to find them sold out everywhere. The frenzy is stoked by newspapers and TV programmes, who stake out toyshops in the hope of catching a riot breaking out. Rumours sweep through social media, with wild claims of new stock seen in corner shops in Rotherham. Parents email bewildered Chinese factory owners to see if they can rustle up some extra stock.

Can you match these toys to the year when they were the hottest item in town?

[1980] [1998] [2004] [1983] [1992] [2006] [1990] [1988]

★ Rubik's Cube   ★ Transformers
★ Cabbage Patch Doll   ★ Teenage Mutant Ninja Turtles
★ Nintendo Wii   ★ Game Boy
★ Robosapien   ★ Furby

Answers: Rubik's Cube, 1980; Cabbage Patch Doll, 1983; Nintendo Wii, 2006; Robosapien, 2004; Transformers, 1990; Teenage Mutant Ninja Turtles, 1988; Game Boy, 1998; Furby, 1992

Did you know?

ELF AND SAFETY

Here are some of the real myths that the government's Health and Safety Executive has had to scotch about Christmas. These myths commonly appear in newspapers and magazine articles, cited as evidence of Grinchy bureaucrats trying to ruin Christmas.

Myth: Workers are banned from putting up Christmas decorations in the office.

Myth: Indoor Christmas lights need a portable appliance test (PAT) every year.

Myth: You can't throw out sweets at pantos.

Myth: Second-hand toys can't be donated to charity shops or hospitals for 'health and safety' reasons.

Myth: Carol singers are a health and safety risk, with over-zealous parish councils and insurers worried about accidents on other people's property.

Myth: Children are banned from throwing snowballs.

Myth: If you clear snow from outside your business or home you are likely to get sued.

Myth: Health and safety prevents people putting coins in Christmas puddings.

HOW TO ...
GET THROUGH A NATIVITY PLAY

Going to see children perform in a Christmas nativity play isn't as straightforward as it might seem. Although the core plot essentially remains the same, embellishments to story and cast can be confusing. This is often compounded by the challenging acting style of children, who may either bellow or whisper like a mini Al Pacino, or suddenly burst into tears for no reason. This guide should help you make head and tail of what's going on.

★ The *dramatis personae* has vastly expanded. Not only do you have shepherds A, B and C (as they are known in the Gospels), but an array of creatures that could include aliens, fleas and snowmen. Be surprised at nothing.

★ Expect more people on stage than in the audience. In the spirit of inclusivity, everyone gets a role (see above) in the nativity play. This means that at the end the whole cast squash together on a dangerously crowded and groaning stage, adding a sense of dramatic jeopardy that may have been missing from the performance itself.

Survive!

★ Just as Shakespeare plays are recast in modern dress and new locations, so too nativity plays, which often take a daring and contemporary approach. Eschewing the traditional Roman-era Bethlehem setting, nativity plays may now be located in modern England or even outer space.

★ Be assured that the baby Jesus is just a doll, so when Mary drops it for the fifth time and one of the Three Kings spills his myrrh bottle on it, no real babies are being harmed.

★ Walking, remembering lines and waving at parents is often too much multitasking for many children. Try to guess which will be the first to fall off the stage.

Weird Traditions

CHRISTMAS QUACKERS

In Sweden Christmas means Donald Duck.

Every year, on Christmas Eve afternoon, half of Sweden sits down in front of the television for a family viewing of the 1958 *Walt Disney Presents* Christmas special, 'From All of Us to All of You.' Or as it is known in Sverige, *Kalle Anka och hans vänner önskar God Jul*: 'Donald Duck and his friends wish you a Merry Christmas.'

Kalle Anka, for short, has been airing without commercial interruption at the same time on Sweden's main public television channel since 1959. When attempts were made in the 1970s to replace the show, the public outcry was so fierce that the broadcasters had to back down and reinstate it, where it has remained ever since.

Games

DECORATE THE TREE

A fun game to use up any wrapping paper, streamers and spare decorations and Christmassy bits and bobs, while ensuring at least two members of the family end up looking completely ridiculous.

You will need: At least three people per team; old wrapping paper, tinsel, streamers and whatever spare bits of decoration you can find lying around; a timer.

HOW TO PLAY

One person from each team is the tree, and the others must decorate them as best they can in one minute. The idea is to wind wrapping paper and streamers around them to cover up as much as possible, then decorate away. The winner is the team that has made the best 'tree' when time is up.

CLEAR OFF, SANTA

Traditionalists may complain that Christmas is becoming increasingly secular, but that doesn't stop it being looked on highly unfavourably in a number of strict religious countries. In fact, historically, it's been banned more times than Uncle Keith from the Christmas Advocaat. Permission to land for Santa's sleigh is currently withheld in the following countries:

Brunei. Sharia law means that Christmas is banned in the sultanate. Fines and jail await those caught celebrating.

Tajikistan. In 2014 the Tajik government banned Father Christmas as he is at odds with its increasingly strict Muslim rule.

Saudi Arabia. As a theocracy governed by Islam, it's no surprise that Christmas isn't welcome here.

North Korea. Very touchy about all organised religion, and especially organized religion that includes holidays, North Korea is so sensitive that when South Korea erected a big Christmas tree near the border they interpreted it as an act of aggressive provocation.

Did you know?

Somalia. Worried about the corruption of its young, Somalia has banned Christmas and New Year celebration at the behest of its Islamic government.

In the past Christmas has been banned in both England (under Cromwell) and the USA, when the Puritans banned it in 1620, renaming it 'Foolstide'.

HOW (NOT) TO ...
WRAP A PRESENT

Present wrapping is a pointless and often degrading task involving huge lengths of infuriatingly fragile and unwieldy paper. By the time they are 35, the average adult has spent 15.7 days of their life trying to find the end of the sellotape.

★ First, try to get someone else to do it. There exist people who actually like wrapping stuff up; there are even YouTube channels for these perverts where they watch someone slowly and provocatively fold and tape gifts. Filth!

★ If you can't find a willing person, then why not break with tradition and give your gifts unwrapped? Insist that you are doing your bit for the environment.

★ If they complain, point out that the three wise men didn't gift wrap their presents to the baby Jesus. Nowhere in the Good Book does it say, 'And lo, they cometh from the East bearing gifts. But these gifts were bare and not wrapped, and the LORD was annoyed. And Mary did tosseth the gifts disdainfully unto the water bucket'.

Survive!

★ You could just buy a gift bag, and just toss the gift into one of those. However, an empty crisp packet turned inside out has a nice shiny silver finish perfect for the festive season and is a fraction of the cost.

★ Shop clever. Only ever buy stuff in shops that wrap it for you. If they won't, move on.

'What I don't like about office Christmas parties is looking for a job the next day.'

PHYLLIS DILLER

CHRISTMAS TURKEY –
SOUTHERN STYLE

Want to enjoy Christmas dinner like a good ol' boy? Then decant the stumphole whisky from the bucket to a jug, put on your favourite festive banjo carols album and go git your turkey. You can forget Delia, Jamie and Nigella (although you can use their recipe books to build up a roaring fire under your drum full of boiling oil if you want) and let's create the Christmas miracle of deep-fried whole turkey. Apparently responsible for 5 deaths, 60 injuries and $10 million worth of damages each year, deep-frying turkey is a macho pastime that can only be done outdoors by those unafraid of risk. Concerns about the healthiness of deep-fried turkey aren't really an issue: if you're the sort of person who's going to cook a 10lb lump of poultry in a drum of boiling oil, calorie-counting probably isn't top of your agenda.

*Christmas
Past*

CHRISTMAS AT WAR

The medieval code of chivalry dictates that quests for
honour and glory should cease for Christmas Day. The most
famous example of arms being set aside is, of course, the
trenches in 1914, when British and German troops put down
their weapons to meet in the middle of no man's land for a
game of football and to exchange tobacco and small tokens.
However, it wasn't like this everywhere up and down the line.
Some units were expressly forbidden from trying to arrange
a temporary armistice and were threatened with court-
martial if they tried to contact the German soldiers.

STOCKING FILLER

The tradition of Christmas stockings is thought to have come from three sisters who were too poor to afford a marriage dowry and were, therefore, doomed to a life of prostitution. They were saved, however, when the wealthy Bishop Saint Nicholas of Smyrna crept down their chimney and generously filled their stockings with gold coins.

The world's largest Christmas stocking measured 32.56 metres long and 14.97 metres wide. It weighed as much as five reindeer and held almost 1,000 presents. It was made by the Children's Society in London on 14 December 2007.

SANTA BY ANY OTHER NAME

A man of many faces – can you match Santa to his country?

- ★ Kerstman
- ★ Viejo Pascuero ('Old Man Christmas')
- ★ Hoteiosho (a god or priest who bears gifts)
- ★ Julenissen ('Christmas gnome')
- ★ Swiety Mikolaj (St. Nicholas)
- ★ Joulupukki
- ★ Père Nöel
- ★ Sheng Dan Lao Ren ('Christmas Old Man')

- ★ Kanakaloka
- ★ Mikulás (St Nicholas)
- ★ Babbo Natale
- ★ Ded Moroz ('Grandfather Frost')
- ★ Jultomten ('Christmas brownie')
- ★ Père Nöel
- ★ Papai Noel
- ★ Weihnachtsmann ('Christmas Man')

55

Answers: Netherlands – Kerstman; Chile – Viejo Pascuero ('Old Man Christmas'); Japan – Hoteiosho (a god or priest who bears gifts); Norway – Julenissen ('Christmas gnome'); Netherlands – Swiety Mikolaj (St. Nicholas); Finland – Joulupukki; France – Pere Nöel; Germany – Sheng Dan Lao Ren ('Christmas Old Man'); Hawaii – Kanakaloka; Hungary – Mikulás (St. Nicholas); Italy – Babbo Natale; Russia – Ded Moroz ('Grandfather Frost'); Sweden – Jultomten ('Christmas brownie'); Poland – Pére Nöel; Brazil – Papai Noel; Germany – Weihnachtsmann ('Christmas Man')

HOW TO ... GET THROUGH CHRISTMAS TRAVEL

'I'm driving home for Christmas,' sang Chris Rea. No doubt because all the trains had been cancelled and only a mad person would consider a long-distance coach journey on Christmas Eve. Travelling at Christmas is so bad that they even made a film about it (*Planes, Trains and Automobiles* – well, strictly speaking it's set at Thanksgiving, but same difference). No one voluntarily sets out on a long trip for Christmas, but if there's definitely no way to get out of it then follow these guidelines:

★ You're not the only one hungover from your work Christmas party! If there's mistletoe at the airport check-ins get ready to kiss your luggage goodbye.

★ Long car journey? Bring a bag of sweets for the children. Don't hand them over, though: every time they misbehave, throw a sweet out of the window.

Survive!

★ Thinking of flying somewhere warm, but want to take a reminder of a white Christmas with you? Don't pack artificial snow, or you may find it mistaken for narcotics and confiscated. No one should spend Christmas with a man pulling on a rubber glove and instructing you to bend over. Unless they want to.

★ Just beyond the half-way point of your journey is the most likely time to realize you have forgotten the presents. Service stations are very well equipped these days, and a Little Waitrose sandwich is a great gift for anyone. See page 106, 'How To … Go Christmas Shopping'.

★ The wise men weren't called wise for nothing. They set off on their Christmas journey three months in advance. Take note!

WAIT A MINUTE

Waits were a musical accompaniment that no one really wanted, rather like a vuvuzela under your bedroom window. From medieval times Waits formed the town band, assembling to blow their motley selection of pipes any time a dignitary visited or the mayor went for a walkabout. Banned by an Act of Parliament in 1835, they still managed to cling on, turning up like an unwanted weird uncle every Christmas to pipe out carols for money. Eventually, to everyone's relief, they seem to have finally admitted defeat and the custom died out around the end of the nineteenth century.

Games

CHRISTMAS CROONERS

Make like David Bowie and Bing Crosby in this Christmas duet game – good for big groups.

You will need: An even number of players; the titles of Christmas songs written down on slips of paper (each song is written down twice on a pair of slips – the same number of slips as there are players); a hat or container to put slips in.

HOW TO PLAY

Each person draws a slip of paper from the hat. Once everyone has a slip of paper they can look at their song without showing it to anyone. Everyone should start humming (not singing) their song at the same time. Each player has to find the other person who is humming the same song as they are. Once they locate them, they hold hands and start singing the song out loud. The first pair to do this are the winners – the last are the losers and can be given a suitable forfeit.

CHRISTMAS CARACAS

In Caracas, the capital of Venezuela, it is the tradition that
everyone who can travels to early-morning church services
on roller skates — roads are even cleared to provide
Christmas worshippers with a safe passage. On their way,
skaters will tug on the ends of long pieces of string tied by
children to their big toes and dangled out of the window.

HOW TO ... KEEP SANTA ALIVE

Your solemn responsibility as a grown-up over Christmas is to KEEP SANTA ALIVE. It sounds like a medical emergency, and in some ways it's just as serious. You don't want to be the person who bursts the Santa bubble; leave that to the horrible kid at school. Every class has one. Instead, you must take every opportunity to perpetuate the belief that a fat man who is a stranger will be visiting the house at night and wandering around, and that this is a good thing, but only on Christmas Eve. If it happens on other days, then we call the nice policeman, don't we?

★ Plan a visit to see Santa in his grotto. This experience alone is enough for most children, and the beard and costume are ample disguise. Even if you recognize Santa as Dave from next door, they won't.

★ On Christmas Eve, take every opportunity to point to the sky and wonder out loud if that moving light is Santa's sleigh, even though you know it's the police helicopter hovering over a massive brawl outside the shopping centre.

Survive!

★ If you don't have a fireplace, remember to make great play out of leaving another way for Santa to get in. Maybe open a window, or leave the back door ajar. Don't forget to close them before you go to bed, in case you do receive a Christmas Eve visit from the anti-Santa who nicks all your presents.

Playlist

WEIRD CHRISTMAS SONGS

Bored of the same old classics at Christmas time? Then try these mind-bending tracks to get your party off with an alternative bang.

★ **'Christmas at Ground Zero'** – Weird Al Yankovic. Where better to celebrate?

★ **'Merry Christmas'** – The Ramones 'don't want to fight tonight'. We can all get on board with that, right?

★ **'The Christmas Unicorn'** – Sufjan Stevens. Because Christmas is the traditional time for unicorns, isn't it?

★ **'Sleigh Ride'** – C3PO and R2D2. In a galaxy far, far away, it's Christmas and it's snowing!

★ **'Christmas in Heaven'** – Monty Python. Angel Santas with fake boobs? Of course!

CHRISTMAS CREEP

Christmas creep is the phenomenon of Christmas coming earlier and earlier each year. Retailers and advertisers work together to try and get you into the spending spirit as soon as they possibly can. Hence the phenomenon of Christmas selection biscuits appearing next to the suntan lotion in the supermarket in mid-August. Taking the metaphorical biscuit was Harrods, who in 2012 opened their festive display 151 days before Christmas Day – on 29 July!

HOW TO ...
SURVIVE A HOLIDAY HANGOVER

Over-indulging in alcohol and Christmas go together like Brussels sprouts and flatulence. These hangover hacks will help you regain your zip after too much festive revelling.

★ As with grief, the most important stage with hangovers is acceptance. Once you recognize that your hangover is your temporary master, and an angry one at that, then you can set about appeasing it. Don't fight it. You'll just feel worse.

★ You've probably drunk unusual Christmas drinks, like liqueurs and eggnog. Be similarly adventurous with your hangover remedies. Maybe Christmas pudding steeped in Alka-Seltzer broth is the answer to your turbulent morning-after stomach?

★ At least there should be a good supply of sugary food on hand. Christmas tree chocolates, Advent calendars and candy canes are all good sources.

★ Avoid a hangover by continuously drinking from early December until New Year. This isn't as dissolute as it sounds. A glass of wine at lunch every day, a few drinks in the evening, a regular nightcap and you're golden. If anyone asks what you are doing, tell them 'because it's Christmas'. But remember, Christmas doesn't end in late March.

THE REAL WENCESLAS

Good King Wenceslas was actually a duke, not a king. In AD 929 Wenceslas of Bohemia (now the Czech Republic) spread Christianity throughout the land. As they do at Christmas, his family got annoyed with him, and his brother and mother chopped Wenceslas up – ironically into bits and pieces, just like you'd chop up winter fuuuu-el.

Bonus Wenceslas joke: How does Good King Wenceslas like his pizza?

Deep and crisp and even.

PASS THE ... COFFINS

In ye olden times, mince pies used to be rectangular in
shape, hence the name 'coffins'. They were also filled
with meat and spices. To celebrate Christmas they were
sometimes formed into little mangers with a pastry baby
Jesus atop. Needless to say, Puritans took a dim view
of what they saw as a malign popish influence on their
baked goods, what with all the pastry idolatry and fancy
decoration, and the elaborate mince pie faded away. After
the Restoration mince pies took on the plainer round shape
we now have, although they were often significantly bigger –
some monsters up to 20lb.

Christmas Past

TINDER – OLDE ENGLANDE STYLE

Young single woman, GSOH, owns own shoes and dress and bonnet, can spin wool, pluck a chicken and work in the fields. Seeking husband.

If a single young lady in the Middle Ages was looking for love, she might well have been advised to follow the Christmas superstition of the Dumb Cake to find 'the one'.

Upon Christmas Eve she should, in absolute silence, prepare a cake but not bake it. She should prick her initials into the top, then leave the cake at her bedroom door and retire for the night. During the night her husband to be would steal in and prick his initials next to hers. In the morning she would bake the cake, see the initials and find her one true love.

CELEBRATE WITH A BANG

The Christmas cracker was invented, of course, by an Englishman. What other nation would so love a gimmick that offers nothing but a muted pop, a terrible joke and a disappointing gift? Tom Smith, a baker, got the concept of paper-encased treats when he visited Paris in the mid-19th century and saw their elegant wrapped bonbons. When he got home he developed the idea, adding a love message and, after painstaking experimentation, a small explosive strip that gives the 'crack' to cracker, or 'cosaque' as they were originally known.

HOW TO ...
MAKE CHARADES MORE FUN

If you can't get out of a family game of charades, why not subtly add these wildcards to the hat to inject a bit of chaos and fun:

Film:
- ★ *Fanny by Gaslight*
- ★ *The Good, the Bad and the Ugly*
- ★ *Dirty Dancing*
- ★ *Free Willy*
- ★ *She's the Man*

Book:
- ★ *Moby Dick*
- ★ *Extremely Loud and Incredibly Close*
- ★ *Diary of a Nobody*

TV:
- ★ *Desperate Housewives*
- ★ *Only Fools and Horses*
- ★ *Orange Is the New Black*

Song:
- ★ 'Cheek to Cheek'
- ★ 'The Thong Song'
- ★ 'Love Machine'

'Nothing's as mean as giving a little child
something useful for Christmas.'

KIN HUBBARD

A CHRISTMAS AFFAIR

Philanderers, beware. Divorce lawyers have pinpointed Christmas as the most likely time of year for people who are having an illicit affair to be discovered in their infidelity. Unfaithful partners, while normally adept at covering their tracks, may lower their guard during the season of goodwill and get caught out. Psychologists have described Christmas Day as a 'perfect storm' for exposing infidelity, with the effects of alcohol, high emotions and temporary separation from secret lovers proving too much for some. It's also a time when people start to do things that they normally wouldn't and say things that they shouldn't, with Christmas parties an especially risky time for bad behaviour.

Food &
Drink

DEALING WITH
A CHRISTMAS GLUT

Food proportions are a perennial Christmas problem. There is always a glut of food you don't want, and a shortage of stuff that you really do. That's why you are still eating your cheddar wheel in June, when the chocolates ran out on Boxing Day. Here's what to do with excess food.

★ Curry it. Anything can be curried, within reason. Turkey curry is the most famous Christmas leftover meal, but curried pigs-in-blankets, curried vegetables and even curried nut roast (for the vegetarian) can work. Just be careful currying sprouts, lest you conjure mighty forces that would power a wind farm.

★ The Christmas cheese mountain can be conquered by throwing a fondue party. This has the twin advantages of melting all surplus cheese into an indistinguishable goop, and also being a Christmassy, Alpine sort of thing to do.

★ You may have some strange, undrinkable booze left. Don't pour it away! It's the perfect gift to bring to a New Year's Eve party where you can palm it off on your host. If the karma of the universe is with you, you'll be giving them back the bottle they palmed off on you for Christmas.

HOW TO ... BUY PRESENTS FOR CHILDREN WHEN YOU DON'T HAVE ANY YOURSELF

Present buying for children can be hard when you are not familiar with their ways and foibles. Long gone are the days when it was simply Meccano or dollies for children under 16, and cigarettes for those over. There is a bewildering array of choice; these simple hints will help you navigate towards the perfect gift.

★ Ask yourself three key questions before setting out to make a purchase: How much do you care about the child? How much do you want to spend? How much do you like their parents? If the answer to all these is 'not much', then great. Just buy the first thing you see.

★ If you really don't like their parents, buy the first thing you see that makes a lot of noise. Preferably something where the batteries can't be removed.

★ If stuck, fall back on your instincts. What would you have liked? If the answer is a simple bag of wooden building bricks, then buy them that. Don't underestimate the pleasure you will derive from playing with those same bricks at home yourself, when the ungrateful child hands them back to you in disgust.

★ Teens: just give them money. Cold, hard cash is what they want. Don't even consider asking them what they are going to spend it on, though. The answer would embarrass both of you.

Weird Traditions

YOU BETTER BE GOOD.
SERIOUSLY

The evil yin to Saint Nicholas' jolly yang, Krampus is a horned, devil-like figure who, during the Christmas season punishes children who have misbehaved, in contrast with Saint Nick, who rewards the well-behaved with gifts. Punishments include being caned with a birch rod, or being stuffed in Krampus' sack to be hauled away to be tortured and eaten. He originates from Austria, but takes bookings from parents across the world who want to instil some fear into their children.

Survive!

HOW TO ...
HAVE A CHRISTMAS LIE-IN

For parents, Christmas Day starts way too early. Demented with excitement, children arise before dawn to see what Santa has brought in the night. Here's how to make your beloved offspring stay in bed until at least it's light outside:

★ Make like Mary and Joseph and wrap your children in swaddling. Tell them that it's part of Christmas tradition to go to bed like baby Jesus. If they can't even move their arms they can't get up at 4am.

★ Change the clocks. Iphones and other technology have made this harder, granted, but with a bit of perserverance it's still possible.

★ Crank up the thermostat. There's a good reason lions in the African savannah sleep in the day – the heat makes them drowsy. Toast your own pride of cubs into slumber.

★ Tell them Santa isn't coming this year.

WHAT DOES YOUR CHRISTMAS TREE SAY ABOUT YOU?

What does your choice of festive sawn-off evergreen reveal about how you like to spend Christmas...?

Tree: Norway Spruce
Old skool, pyramid in shape, with a tendency to drop needles, often before you get home.

You are: A hipster traditionalist, where doing things correctly takes precedence over practicality or enjoyment. Nothing takes away the warm glow of smugness, not even the fact that you'll be staring at a brown skeleton of bare twigs by Boxing Day.

Tree: Nordmann Fir
Dark green foliage and soft leaves, suited to fewer decorations.

You are: Sensible and pragmatic. Maybe a bit dull. This tree is a popular choice with the ability to hold its needles well. Some might call this a vanilla tree for vanilla people, but who cares? It's maintenance free, leaving all the more time for booze and sweets and telly.

Tree: Blue Spruce

Elegant, with natural blue foliage. Rarely seen outside lifestyle TV programmes and photo shoots in style magazines.

You are: A metropolitan poseur. At least 90 per cent of the joy of having this tree is knowing that no one else has got one. In fact, you had to order it online last June at enormous cost from a source that you are keeping a jealously guarded secret.

Tree: Fraser Fir

Leaner in shape with much denser foliage, ideal in a baronial hall. A tree only available if you grow it yourself, usually on your Scottish estate. Should be adorned with nothing but ill-matched ornaments that have been handed down through the family over the years — you'd never do anything so vulgar as to buy decorations.

You are: The Queen.

Did you know?

TOP-GROSSING CHRISTMAS MOVIES

Here's a list of the highest-grossing Christmas films, by worldwide takings. Because nothing says Christmas like Macaulay Culkin. Or Bruce Willis in a vest.

1. **Home Alone** (1990) $476,684,675

2. **Home Alone 2: Lost in New York** (1992) $358,994,850

3. **How the Grinch Stole Christmas** (2000) $345,141,403

4. **A Christmas Carol** (2009) $325,286,646

5. **The Polar Express** (2004) $307,514,317

6. **Love, Actually** (2003) $246,942,017

7. **Die Hard 2: Die Harder** (1990) $240,031,094.

8. **Elf** (2003) $220,443,451

9. **The Santa Clause** (1994) $189,833,357

10. **The Santa Clause 2: Mrs Clause** (2002) $172,855,065

NON-PC CHRISTMAS GIFTS

Here are some real life, rather questionable gifts from days gone by:

★ Junior smoker's kit made of chocolate: pipe, cigars, cigarettes. As sold to children as recently as the 1980s. Chocolate iron lung not included.

★ A vacuum cleaner, especially for her. According to the advertising of the time, 'Christmas morning she'll be happier with a Hoover.'

★ A tea caddy shaped like a gun shell – popular in 1915 for mothers as a reminder of their boy serving in the trenches.

★ The homeless 'American Girl' doll! One of a series of 'American Girl' dolls, Gwen can be yours for $95.

★ A ouija board. Sporadically popular over the last 100 years, and most recently in 2014 following the release of the film *Ouija*. Because what's Christmas if it isn't about family getting together? Even if they're dead.

HOW TO ...
SIT THROUGH A PANTOMIME

The chief pleasure of going to the panto at Christmas is that you know exactly what you are going to get. There are no surprises: a familiar story, cross-dressing actors and a dame. This is what we know and like. No one wants to go to see an experimental silent modern dance interpretation of *Mother Goose*.

There are some rules about panto-going. Follow these, and you'll be guaranteed a satisfying experience. Oh yes you will!

★ There is a correct time to go to the panto. Although the season starts in November, this is too early. Equally, going to a panto after New Year's Day is a miserable experience. Everyone is thinking about going back to work or school, and the actors on stage by this point openly despise each other. Optimal panto time is between 10 and 30 December.

Survive!

★ Don't sit too near the front, and never on the end of the row. This is the location of maximum jeopardy for being plucked from the audience and publicly humiliated by the Dame. Unless, of course, being abused by a fat man in make-up and a dress is your thing. In which case, book early to ensure you get your kicks.

★ Ensure any children you are taking gorge themselves on sweets and ice cream to the point that they feel sick. The panto experience is only enhanced by the anxiety of wondering if the small person next to you is about to vomit like an erupting volcano.

SNOW-WOMEN

According to *Guinness World Records*, the biggest snowman
ever built was in Maine in the USA, and stood 37.21m tall. In
fact, it was actually a snow-woman named Olympia after State
senator Olympia Snowe. She was built in a little over a month
and was dressed in a 100-foot scarf, had 27-foot evergreen
trees for arms, and eyelashes made from old skis.

Did you know?

WHAT IS BOXING DAY?

Boxing day, or 26 December as it's known outside the UK and Commonwealth, is a bit of a mystery. Historians debate its origins. The tradition of wealthy households giving gifts (often in a box, hence the name) to tradesmen, servants and local poor people originated in Victorian England. This may be why employers still give a bonus at Christmas time, too. But others hold that the name derives from the Middle Ages, when alms boxes were placed in church to collect donations for the poor, which were distributed on the day after Christmas. Of course, we now know that the true purpose of Boxing Day is when you repackage all your unwanted gifts, 'boxing' them up to take back to the shops.

'The lovely thing about Christmas is that it's compulsory, like a thunderstorm, and we all go through it together.'

GARRISON KEILLOR

CHRISTMAS BREAK UP

Analysis of Facebook posts revealed that two weeks before Christmas is one of the two most popular times for couples to split up. But Christmas Day itself is the least likely day to break up. Unless, of course, you're watching *EastEnders*, where Christmas isn't Christmas without a healthy dollop of splits, violence and other assorted misery.

But even if you make it through Christmas, you might still find yourself dumped. New Year is a popular time to break up, as New Year's Eve indiscretions come to light, or people decide to make a fresh start. In fact, the period between New Year and Valentine's Day is the most popular period for break-ups in the whole year.

HOW TO ... PLAY BOARD GAMES

The board game has become a staple Christmas cliché, if not reality. How many people really sit down in front of the Monopoly board just because it's Christmas? The whole idea is misconceived – if you don't play board games the rest of the year, why should you, stuffed with food and slightly tipsy, want to play now? But if you are compelled by others, these hints should get you through.

★ Never volunteer to take any responsible roles. Avoid being the banker, dealer, chief, prison guard or whoever is in authority in the game you are playing. The less important you are, the easier you can drop out quickly!

★ Games with huge instructions books are seldom fun. If someone opens the new game they got for Christmas and pulls out a volume the thickness of an average paperback, make your excuses and get out. Otherwise you'll be stuck in an excruciatingly drawn-out game that keeps stopping while the rule book is consulted.

Survive!

★ Don't play with these types of people: ones who bring their own dice; anyone who insists on being a certain character, i.e. the boot in Monopoly; people who make like they're in a casino every time it's their go, blowing on the dice and shouting nonsense about lucky 7; and known bad losers, who have only just recovered their emotional equilibrium after losing Cluedo last Christmas.

THE 12 CLICHÉS OF CHRISTMAS

Part of the appeal of Christmas is the comfort of familiarity. But familiar can quickly become cliché, especially when it's drenched in mawkish sentimentality. Nowhere is this more apparent than in Christmas adverts, where just because an idea has been done 100 times, doesn't mean it can be recycled again and again. Make up some bingo cards and see who can tick off these stale clichés to try to keep you awake during the terrible Christmas TV.

★ A huge, golden turkey, with a single slice cut out.

★ Snow. Abundant, fat, thick snow. The likes of which is really seldom seen outside of Christmas cards or Siberia.

★ The adult child returning to the old family home. That's the same family home they couldn't wait to get out of to Uni a few months ago.

★ Perfect square presents, wrapped with a bow. Do these even really exist?

Games

★ A showstopper ad, featuring an old 80s indie hit slowed down, stripped bare and breathily murmured by a gamine chanteuse.

★ Roaring fire in the hearth, as if everyone lives like a medieval baron.

★ Twinkly old Grandpa, asleep after dinner. Faking it, no doubt, to get out of the washing up.

★ Dad hogging the kids' new toys.

★ Stressed mum in kitchen. Bonus points if the turkey too big for oven cliché is there, too.

★ Jolly carollers, who seem to know all the words. And are entirely sober.

★ Animals. Prime suspects are penguin, polar bear, family dog. Often, bizarrely, in combinations nature never intended.

★ Children fast asleep on Christmas Eve. Yeah, right.

RUDOLPH THE
RED-NOSED ADVERTISING GIMMICK

Rudolph the red-nosed reindeer was invented for a US firm's Christmas promotion in 1938. Looking around for a new idea for a book they could give away to children at Christmas, a young employee called Robert L. May came up with the idea of a young reindeer whose glowing nose could lead Santa's sleigh through dark and wintry storms. In the first year the company gave away 2.5 million copies of *Rudolph the Red Nosed Reindeer*, and a Christmas legend was born.

A FINGER-LICKIN' YULE

Traditional Christmas dinner in Japan is ... KFC with all the trimmings! The Colonel carried out such a successful advertising campaign in 1974 that the Japanese, who didn't generally celebrate the festive season, went wild for Kurisumasu ni wa Kentakkii or Kentucky for Christmas. Now it's so popular that queues stretch out of the door, and people place their Christmas order up to two months in advance. The most popular product is the Christmas Party Barrel – a selection of fried goodness to share with friends and family at this special time of the year.

GLUHWEIN

Gluhwein, or, as we Brits prefer, mulled wine, is a drink
with history, popular with well-to-do medieval households
to show off their wealth and generosity. Sadly, this noble
tradition isn't always respected by your local pub, who serve
their own 'mulled wine' tasting of pot-pourri straight from
the microwave in a plastic cup. But done right it can be a
great thing.

If you want to go more hardcore, the Swedes have their own
version called Glogg, which is basically Gluhwein on steroids.
The ingredients are pretty similar, but include bourbon, rum
or vodka. Its signature tasting note is cough syrup. Yum. Hic.

INGREDIENTS:

(No exact quantities here –
just go with your instincts. It
shouldn't burn like mouthwash,
but it should have a bit of a
spicy kick.)

A bottle of red wine
an orange
a lemon
sugar
ginger wine
cinnamon
cloves
nutmeg

Food &
Drink

METHOD

1. Put the wine in the pan with the lemon peel, juice of the orange, sugar and spices. Heat up, stirring until sugar has dissolved.

2. Pour in ginger wine, to taste. Heat it all up, but take care not to boil it and thereby lose all the alcohol.

3. Drink it.

HOW TO ...
SPEND CHRISTMAS ABROAD

Many fantasize about Christmas abroad. For the weather, or simply to escape from all that it entails at home. However, it can be a fairly disconcerting experience, especially if you are somewhere hot while in all the shops there are pictures of snowy scenes and Santa on his sleigh. Make the most of your Christmas abroad by following these tips:

★ When in Rome. If the locals have an obvious tradition, try and join in and have a truly local experience. Just push your way into someone's home on Christmas Day for lunch. Either they'll welcome you in the spirit of goodwill to all men, or chase you from their premises with a knife. Either way it will be memorable.

★ Do you have an overwhelming urge to hear 'I Wish It Could be Christmas Every Day'? Simply bang your head on the nearest hard object repeatedly until it passes.

Survive!

★ Banish thoughts of nostalgia and homesickness by relaxing on a sun lounger, ordering a cocktail and admiring the azure sky. Then imagine your extended family crowded into a stuffy living room, bathed in the lingering scent of grey boiled Brussels, watching *The Snowman*.

★ Christmas in a hot country is always odd. Fairy lights look tacky when it's light until 9pm, and cooking a turkey in 30-degree heat is always going to be a stupid idea. Maybe give Christmas a miss …

HANG YOUR SHINING SWASTIKA FROM THE HIGHEST BOUGH

Strange but true: the Nazis tried to bring Christmas into line with their own ideology. Firstly, Saint Nicholas was replaced by the Germanic god Odin, who wore a hat and rode about on a big horse with a sack of gifts. Then the traditional star was replaced with a swastika at the top of the tree, which was itself rebranded as the 'light tree'. It's didn't stop there: in an attempt to remove Christian associations with Christmas, Jesus in the manger was replaced by a garden full of wooden animals, and catalogues of children's toys featured chocolate SS guards, tanks and machine guns. Cheery!

'I trust Christmas brings to you its
traditional mix of good food and violent
stomach cramp.'

EBENEZER BLACKADDER,
BLACKADDER'S CHRISTMAS CAROL

HOW TO ... CELEBRATE CHRISTMAS FOR THE HEALTH FANATIC

If you're sworn off sugar, a carb-dodger, or in training for an ultra-desert-assault-course-triathlon then Christmas is a difficult time. Not only is there lots of unhealthy food and booze around, but days are short, meaning it's harder to get outside and run around. This is probably what your Christmas day looks like:

5AM: Wake up before children. Do 50 silent push-ups in darkness, trying not to wake your partner.

7AM: Prepare breakfast. Smoked salmon and champagne for family. Bran and diluted almond milk for you. It is Christmas, after all.

9AM: Open gifts with family. Note that your partner looks less than pleased with the running shoes and vest you got them.

10AM: Make a big show of noticing the rubbish needs to go out. Use opportunity to go for quick five-mile run.

1PM: Christmas lunch. Allow yourself 20ml of wine. Check heart rate – dangerously elevated to almost 40bpm. Swear off alcohol for evermore.

3PM: Games time! Veto Kerplunk! and instead attempt to engage family in competitive squat thrust competition. When this fails, challenge yourself instead to beat your personal best.

4PM: Filled with self-loathing after succumbing to three Christmas tree chocolates, go online to see if there are any Boxing Day triathlons you can enter.

9PM: Go to bed early wrapped in bin bag to sweat out any toxins. Dream about being chased by an enormous mince pie that wants to kill you.

Christmas
Past

CHRISTMAS WAS A RIOT

William the Conqueror (or William the Bastard, depending
on how you view the French. Or people called William) was
crowned in Westminster Abbey on Christmas Day 1066. The
business of quelling the English completed, the ceremony
to pronounce him king began on the 25th. The crown was
put on William's head, and all the assembled nobles and
obsequious hangers-on started cheering loudly. Unfortunately
the guards outside thought this was a rebellion flaring up
and sprang into action, which involved burning down all the
houses in the area, totally destroying most of that part of
London in the process.

Did you know?

THE GIFT THAT KEEPS ON GIVING

Paul McCartney is estimated to get £250,000 each year in royalties for his song 'Wonderful Christmas Time'. Cunningly, Paul wrote the song, played all the instruments and produced it himself, meaning he doesn't have to give a piece of the royalty pie to anyone else. This one song on its own earns him nearly as much each year as his Beatles royalties.

Ding dong merrily indeed!

HOW TO ...
GO CHRISTMAS SHOPPING

Christmas is a time of fantasy, where TV adverts and magazines carry endless perfect scenes: the snow gently falling on Christmas Eve; the happy family gathered in front of the fire; a huge pile of perfectly wrapped presents under the tree. Nowhere is the difference between this and reality more stark than in the shopping for presents – the most fist-clenchingly enraging bit of the whole Christmas fandango.

In theory, it has never been easier to sort out Christmas presents now there's online shopping. Set aside a few hours in late November, click away, and all your gifts will be delivered to your front door well before the 25th. Why, then, does the afternoon of Christmas Eve find anxiously sweating people desperately charging round the shops buying anything they can lay their hands on? The answer is, of course, that Christmas shopping is *hard*. Who knows what people really want? Even if you've lived with them for 20 years, this can be impossible. For people you don't know

Survive!

so well, it's even tougher. What *does* cousin Keith like? So instead of committing, we put off buying stuff until we realize that we've missed the last guaranteed delivery dates from Amazon and are forced out to brave the shops.

The result of all this is the classic Christmas 'that'll do' phenomenon. Snooker cue for Mum? That'll do. A cravat for little Johnny? He may be only 8, but still. That'll do. A satnav for Grandma's mobility scooter? That'll do. Returning home with a motley selections of gifts, you may experience some buyer's remorse. But on Christmas Day, when you open your set of steak knives, photo history of the watermills of East Anglia and luxury padded coat hanger, you'll realize that everyone else has been just as disorganized as you.

Did you know?

THANKS ... BUT NO THANKS

It's estimated that one in four Christmas presents is unwanted. The most returned gifts are:

★ Clothing

★ Jewellery and watches

★ Shoes

★ Books

This list begs the question, what do people actually keep? Women are more likely to be gift returners than men, and one in three people say they will travel a bit further away in case they are spotted returning their unwanted pressies.

TRUE OR NOT?

This game is useful as a not-so-subtle way of letting people really know what you thought of their present last year.

You will need: Players – any number, but the more the better. Paper, pens.

HOW TO PLAY

Each player has a list of all the other players' names, with a space next to each of them. Go round in turn to each player, who has to say what their worst Christmas presents ever were. Each player must give three presents – two of which should be true and one a lie. Everyone should write down the present they think is made up. Each player then reveals which of their answers were true, and which the false one was. The player who spots the most lies wins.

Christmas
Past

TEUTONIC TINSEL TUSSLES

German churches in the eighteenth century had to take the extreme step of banning Christmas midnight mass in towns across the land. Highly popular gatherings, the congregation would pack in after a convivial evening taking liquid refreshment in the local tavern. Services often descended into near riots and mass brawls were not uncommon. Outside the church was even worse, as revellers careered between church and hostelry, fighting and carousing in a most unholy manner as they went.

Food & Drink

HOW TO MAKE A SNOWBALL

A seasonal favourite, the Snowball is a Christmas cocktail that brings with it a bit of 70s glitz and old-fashioned glamour – especially if it has a sparkler stuck in it, which it definitely should have. It includes Advocaat, so if you've got a bottle that you're struggling to get rid of, this is the answer. Made right, you can experience the 'Snowball effect', the warm glow of good cheer that only an egg-based drink can bring.

INGREDIENTS:

1 scoop ice cubes
2 shots Advocaat
½ shots lime cordial
½ shots sherry
lemonade, to top up

METHOD

Put into a tall glass the ice cubes, then pour over the Advocaat, sherry and lime juice juice before topping up with lemonade. Serve, with a sparkler.

HOW TO ...
CHOOSE THE TREE

Choosing the Christmas tree can be a fraught process. Get it wrong and you'll feel the disapproval for all twelve days of Christmas, and probably beyond that too.

★ You might fancy a mighty tree, but too big and you'll struggle to get it home and into the house, where it will then sit with branches unhappily bent against the ceiling. And do you really have enough decorations?

★ However, too small just looks mean, and makes you appear half-hearted and begrudging about the whole thing. If it's smaller than a nearby pot plant you may have a problem ...

★ Before circa 1990 there was only one type of real tree that everyone could buy: the kind that when you slammed the front door all the needles fell off. Now, depending on your budget and Instagram aspirations, you can get all sorts of species of fir.

★ Or you could of course give in and get an artificial tree, despite their associations with sad bachelor flats, cheap municipal displays and slapdash gestures towards the season in shops. It might seem like a cheaper option, but by next December you'll have lost it in the back of the garage anyway.

Weird Traditions

SIMPLY HAVANA WONDERFUL CHRISTMAS TIME

Christmas was officially abolished in Cuba by the communist government to apparently avoid festivities disrupting the vital sugar harvest. Although Fidel Castro did reinstate Christmas in 1997, it's largely been a muted affair, mainly because no one under 40 has experienced it and really knows what to do. Even today, Christmas remains a day of low significance for many Cubans.

'Aren't we forgetting the true meaning of this day – the birth of Santa?'

BART SIMPSON

Christmas Past

CHRISTMAS CHEER – PURITAN STYLE

In 1644, Oliver Cromwell's parliament banned Christmas on the grounds that it wasn't mentioned in the Bible. The link between ancient pagan revels and Christmas was too much for hard-core Puritans to bear. They denounced Christmas as 'Satan's working day' and the 'Antichrist's Mass'. Mince pies were banned! This sorry state of affairs persisted until 1660, when to most people's relief the monarchy was restored and 'party king' Charles II reinstated Christmas.

FAIRY LIGHT FRENZY

All things in moderation is a fine maxim, but when it comes to Christmas light displays, less is definitely not more for some. It's a curious sweet spot of alpha-male competitiveness (because it's always men who go in for light installations that can be seen from Mars), DIY electrical tinkering and a frankly high camp commitment to twinkly lights and gaudy over-decoration.

Consider Mr Dave Richards of Canberra, Australia, who set a world record by somehow cramming 518,838 lights onto his tree.

Or Mr Timothy Gay and family, from New York, who went bigger and better and set the world record for most lights on a residential property of 601,736!

Britain's Brailsford brothers, by contrast, only managed a modest 50,000 lights, although their Bristol display has helped to raise more than £30,000 for charity over the years.

COOK THE PERFECT SPROUT

Avoid the rotten stench of drains from the kitchen when cooking sprouts by not over-boiling the little buggers. Too much cooking makes them release their sulphurous compounds that result in the unmistakable 'eau de fart' aroma. Here's a recipe that should convert even the most sprout-phobic. Remember to cut a cross in the bottom to keep out the devil!

INGREDIENTS:

three thick rashers of bacon (preferably smoked)
500g of trimmed sprouts
100g peeled chestnuts
about 40g – or a big blob – butter

METHOD

1. Cook the sprouts in a pan of boiling water for five minutes (don't overcook!). Drain and run the under the cold tap straight away in a colander or sieve.

2. Fry the bacon in a hot frying pan without any oil for ten minutes until it's crisp. Take it out with a slotted spoon, leaving the fat behind.

3. Add chestnuts to the pan, stir to coat in the fat and fry until they are beginning to colour. Add them to the bowl with the bacon to cool.

4. Put the sprouts in the frying pan with half the butter. Keep the pan quite hot but make sure you are only singeing the outside of the sprouts – not burning them. When they are hot through and tender, add the bacon and chestnuts back into the pan. Season with black pepper and stir until warmed through.

5. Tip into a warm serving dish, then dot the butter over to melt. Toss through and serve. And bingo! Not a sweaty, limp sprout in sight!

Christmas
Past

MISERABLE CHRISTMAS

Scots? Dour? Surely not! The case for the prosecution:
Christmas Day only became a national holiday in Scotland
in 1958, and Boxing Day had to wait until 1974. They had
previous form, though. The strict Calvinist religious grip
that took hold north of the border in the sixteenth century
meant that the Scots had practically stamped out 'popish'
Christmas festivities almost a century before the soft
Puritans down south followed suit.

As a result, Christmas in Scotland was on something of a
back-burner for 400 years. One effect of this was to put
the emphasis for celebrations on New Year, or Hogmanay,
instead of Christmas. For many Scots, New Year is still
firmly *the* big celebration of the year.

HAVE A POLITICALLY CORRECT CHRISTMAS

The University of Texas was criticized for its Grinch-like guidelines, aimed at removing Christmas from the festive season. They recommended holiday parties should have no emphasis on religion or culture, but rather 'build upon workplace relationships and team morale'. The school said parties should never include religious or cultural games.

Additionally, they said, if gifts were exchanged or planned, calling it 'Secret Santa' wasn't appropriate. Instead, the exchange should be referred to in a more general way, such as 'practical joke gift exchange' or 'secret gift exchange'.

HOW TO ...
BE A MASSIVE FOOD SNOB

Christmas provides an excellent opportunity for one-upmanship and snobbery for foodies. Not only are there obscure and challenging foods from around the world that can be incorporated into your festive dining, there's also the not-to-be-missed opportunity of rubbing salt (pink Himalayan, of course) into the wounds as your share your feast with other foodies via your blog.

July: Time to source your rare-breed ptarmigan that you are going to stuff with snipe. You know this year friends are serving unneutered cockerel from France, so you need to go one better.

8am, Christmas Day: Awake, and breakfast on single-estate bacon with a goose's egg. Watch children eat coco pops, and shudder.

9am: Family open presents, while you set about preparing dinner. First job is to peel the Luxembourg sprouts. Brussels sprouts are so inferior.

11am: Put bird in the oven. Family have complained it's not much bigger than a blackbird, but you have told them its exquisite taste means you only need one tiny slice each.

Survive!

Midday: Open eight bottles of carefully selected wine – one for each course you intend to serve – so they can 'breathe'.

3pm: Serve dinner. Of course, no one can touch the food until you have photographed it all for social media.

3.30pm: Allow family to finally eat. When they complain it has gone cold, explain to them that it is actually the optimal temperature to experience the full range of textures and tastes.

4.30pm: Spend two hours alone in your bedroom post lunch uploading photos to your blog and writing a detailed description of your menu.

8pm: After quality time with family go back to check blog comments. You are crushed when someone called 'Gourmetman23' calls your menu derivative and obvious. Go to bed, weeping, with a bottle of vintage Sauternes.

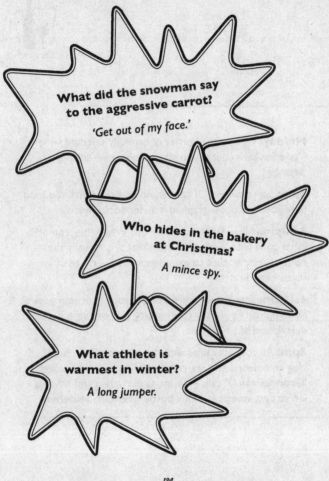

What did the snowman say
to the aggressive carrot?

'Get out of my face.'

Who hides in the bakery
at Christmas?

A mince spy.

What athlete is
warmest in winter?

A long jumper.

Games

TEAM WRAPPING

This game involves teamwork, clear thinking and a steady hand with the scissors.

You will need: Teams made up of two players; a box or similar item to wrap; wrapping stuff – paper, scissors, sticky tape, a ribbon

HOW TO PLAY

The two people on each team will need to stand side by side with one hand free and the other around the waist of their partner. The object of the game is to see which pair of joined 'twins' can wrap their present fastest. You'll need a few other people to be the judges – first to make sure that they have wrapped correctly and nicely, and second to time them for the fastest 'twin' gift wrappers.

CHRISTMAS CARDS

Although the Christmas card may be dying out, we still send on average 17 each. Can the card make a comeback in the face of email, SMS and Facebook? Or will we just end up group texting a Christmas tree emoticon to everyone in our address book? Here are some things you probably don't know about the humble Christmas card.

★ Christmas cards were originally written by schoolboys practising their writing skills. They would take them home and present these handmade cards to their parents.

★ The commercial Christmas card was invented in 1846 by Sir Henry Cole, the chief organizer of the Great Exhibition, pioneer of the penny post and founder of the V&A Museum.

★ Werner Erhard of San Francisco set a world record for sending 62,824 Christmas cards in December 1975.

★ A Christmas card sent by Sir Henry sold for a
world record £20,000 in 2001. It was sent to his
grandmother and is hand-coloured by the London
illustrator John Calcott Horsley. It is considered the
first Christmas card, one of a batch of only 1,000
that were made.

★ Women buy and send over 85% of all Christmas
cards.

HOW TO ...
MAKE IT OUT THE OTHER SIDE

When it comes to finishing Christmas, some people seem to find it easier than others to bid farewell to the festive season. Some have their tree stripped and thrown out on Boxing Day, while others cling on, leaving their decorations up and living on a diet of sweets and alcohol for as long as they possibly can. Here's how to exit the season gracefully.

★ If you've done Christmas justice, then your corpulent frame and exhausted liver should be positively welcoming an austere January of kale juice and early nights. The harder you celebrate Christmas, the easier it is to let it go.

★ Twelfth Night is officially the last day of Christmas when decorations must come down and everything be packed away until next year. This is often when a lot of people also go back to work after their break, creating a uniquely depressing double-whammy. At least you can comfort yourself that you've got one of the most depressing days of the year out of the way early.

★ If you really can't bear to end it, then take the immortal advice of Wizard literally and make it Christmas every day. Some people actually do this – dining on turkey for 365 days a year and living in a permanently decorated house. Or you could move to the town of North Pole, in Alaska, where it really is Christmas every day. Choose between Santa Claus Lane, St Nicholas Drive, Snowman Lane or Kris Kringle Drive, where the streetlights are striped liked candy canes and you can find the world's biggest statue of Santa Claus.

Christmas Past

COLD, COLD CHRISTMAS

Where does the ideal of a white and snowy Christmas come from? After all, Bethlehem is in the Middle East and averages around 11°C in December, far too warm for snow. The answer lies with the Victorians, and the climate they lived in.

When the classic stories about Christmas, like *A Christmas Carol* and 'The Night Before Christmas', were written the Northern Hemisphere was still in what is now called the Little Ice Age. This ran, roughly, between about 1450 and 1850. Temperatures were 1–2 degrees lower, producing longer, colder, snowier winters. This was the period when the Thames would freeze over so thickly that fairs would be held on the ice. Writers like Charles Dickens were used to seeing a wintry landscape, and built this into their stories, and the link between Christmas and snow became established.

'Be careful with drinking this Christmas. I got so drunk last night I found myself dancing in a cheesy bar ... Or, as you like to call it, a delicatessen.'

SEAN HUGHES

BUMPER CHRISTMAS QUIZ!

1. What was the name of Scrooge's late business partner?

2. In which ocean will you find Christmas Island?

3. Name the three wise men.

4. Who is the servant of Cinderella's father and is also Cinderella's friend?

5. Where does the Queen traditionally spend Christmas?

6. What Christmas item takes its name from the old French word *estincelle*, meaning spark?

7. Who composed 'Auld Lang Syne'?

8. If you were born on Christmas Day, what's your star sign?

9. How many Lords a-leaping are there in 'The 12 Days of Christmas'?

10. What does the Brassica oleracea gemmifera give us?

11. In Cockney rhyming slang what are 'eyes' called?

12. In the rhyme 'Christmas is coming', who is getting fat?

13. Which act besides the Beatles is the only other act to have three consecutive Christmas number one singles?

14. In which pantomime do Maid Marion and Robin Hood appear?

15. Under the rule of the White Witch it is always winter but never Christmas – in which fictional country?

16. Which three dimensional puzzle, sold by Ideal Toys, was the most popular Christmas gift in 1980?

17. A year contains 365 days. On what number day does Christmas Day fall?

18. What is the name of the elf played by Will Ferrell in the 2003 film *Elf*?

19. What type of pet is 'Santa's Little Helper' in *The Simpsons*?

20. Which socialist state officially ceased to exist on 25 December 1991?

21. Who tried to steal Christmas from Whoville?

22. What country does turkey originate from?

23. In the song 'I Saw Mummy Kissing Santa Claus', where did Mummy tickle Santa Claus?

24. On what feast day did Good King Wenceslas step out?

25. After fleeing Bethlehem, where did Mary, Joseph and Jesus go?

26. Two of Santa's reindeer are named after the weather. What are they?

27. What country gifts the tree that stands in London's Trafalgar Square every year?

28. Stollen is the traditional Christmas fruit cake of which country?

29. What tree did the partridge sit in?

30. Which country exports the most Christmas trees in the world?

Answers: 1. Jacob Marley; 2. The Indian Ocean; 3. Balthazar, Gaspar and Melchior; 4. Buttons; 5. Balmoral, in Scotland; 6. Tinsel; 7. Robert Burns; 8. Capricorn; 9. 10; 10. Brussels sprouts; 11. Mince pies; 12. The goose; 13. The Spice Girls (bonus points if you can name their singles; '2 become 1'; 'Too Much'; 'Goodbye'); 14. Babes in the Wood; 15. Narnia; 16. Rubik's cube; 17. 359; 18. Buddy Hobbs; 19. A dog; 20. Union of Soviet Socialist Republics (USSR); 21. The Grinch; 22. The USA; 23. 'Underneath his beard so snowy white'; 24. The feast of Stephen; 25. Egypt; 26. Donner, which means thunder in German, and Blitzen, which means lightning; 27. Norway; 28. Germany; 29. Pear tree; 30. Canada

JONATHAN SWAN claims to be Santa's Number 1 helper. He currently lives in London, where he spends his time roasting chestnuts and driving a one-horse open sleigh, despite repeated warnings from the police to desist.